Drumset 101

(A Contemporary Approach to Playing the Drums)

Dave Black & Steve Houghton

Includes:

- **Groove Patterns**
- **Snare Drum & Bass Drum Independence**
- **Drum Fills in Context**
- **Written Charts for Every Tune**
- **A Play-Along CD with 40 Multi-Stylistic Tracks**

Alfred Publishing Co., Inc.
PO Box 10003
Van Nuys, CA, 91406

Alfred

alfred.com

© 2007 by Alfred Publishing Co., Inc.
All rights reserved. Printed in USA.
ISBN-10: 0-7390-4693-4
ISBN-13: 978-0-7390-4693-7

Cover photo: Karen Miller

contents

About the CD

The CD contains most of the exercises and all of the tunes included in this book, so you may listen and play along with them. On many of the tracks, the drums will fade out so you can play along with the song on your own, and sometimes the drums will fade back in towards the end of the song. The CD tracks also serve as drum models to help strengthen time keeping, improve ensemble playing, clarify phrasing and expand your knowledge of styles.

choosing a drumset
to use with this book

If you have completed a beginning snare drum method (such as *Alfred's Drum Method*, Book 1), you are now ready to move on to *Drumset 101* and play a basic four-piece drumset. Although most standard sets include an additional mounted tom-tom, we have left it out of this book for the purpose of simplicity. Once you are comfortable with the material in this book, an additional mounted tom-tom may be added.

The Throne

Let's start with the drum stool, called the *throne*. The height should allow a comfortable sitting position, so that your thighs are parallel to the floor or angled slightly downward. When you place your feet on the foot pedals, your legs should be slightly past a 45-degree angle.

The Basic Drumset Setup

The basic four-piece drumset includes a bass drum, snare drum, mounted tom-tom, floor tom-tom, ride cymbal, crash cymbal, and hi-hat.

The drumset should be set up so that you are comfortable! When you sit on the drum throne, the drums and cymbals should be within easy reach, much like your plate, knife, and fork are within easy reach when you are sitting at the dinner table. So, let's "sit at the table."

The Snare Drum

The snare drum should be positioned about waist level. If the drum is too low, it will limit the use of your hands. When

using the matched grip, the drum should be flat or slanted slightly downward and toward you. Avoid tension.

The Tom-Tom

A mounted tom-tom should be positioned so there are no large gaps in height between the drumheads. It should also be tilted slightly towards you so the drumstick clears the

rim when striking the head. This will make the movements between the snare drum and the tom-tom smooth.

The Floor Tom-Tom

The floor tom-tom should be positioned to the right of the snare drum (for a right-handed player) at approximately the same height. You may angle the drum slightly towards you or the snare drum so the drumstick clears

the rim when striking the head. This will make the movements from the snare drum (or mounted tom-tom) to the floor tom-tom smooth.

The Ride Cymbal

The ride cymbal should be placed to the right of your drumset. It should be positioned so that when you extend your arm (like for a handshake), the stick will strike two to four inches from the edge of the cymbal.

Tuning Your Drums

Proper tuning of your drums is important to achieve a good sound. There are many things to consider before tuning your drums. First, make sure your drumheads are in good shape. If they're not, replace them with new heads. Before selecting a particular type of drumhead, it is important to decide which style of music you will be playing (rock, jazz, country, R&B, etc.).

Drumheads are held in place by wooden or metal *counterhoops*, and are adjusted by threaded rods. Tightening or loosening these rods will alter the tension of the heads.

The *batter head* is the top head of the snare drum, the top head of a tom-tom, and the back head of the bass drum. It is best to start with the batter head when tuning your drums.

Tension your drums so they sound high to low as you move from the snare drum to the bass drum.

When tuning your drums, we recommend using the *cross-tension system* because it maintains even tensioning around the drum during the entire tuning process. To tune your drums using this method, start with tension rod number 1 and tighten each screw one twist of the wrist at a time until the drumhead feels firm. Be sure not to tension any lug more than the others. Tap the head with a drumstick about two inches in from each rod to be certain the pitch is consistent around the drum. If it is not, adjust individual tension rods as needed.

Cross-Tension System of Tensioning

For a more detailed reference guide on tuning, please refer to *How to Tune Your Drums* (Alfred item 20426).

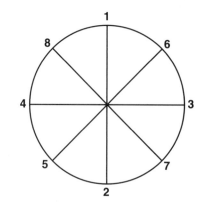

4

the drumset

Basic Four-Piece Setup

Crash Cymbal

Ride Cymbal

Mounted Tom-Tom

Snare Drum

Hi-Hat Cymbals

Throne

Floor Tom-Tom

Hi-Hat Stand

Cymbal Stand

Bass Drum Pedal

Bass Drum

Drumset Notation

Each line and space of the staff designates a particular drum or cymbal.

Crash Cymbal

Cross-Stick

Ride Cymbal with Stick (R.C.)
Hi-Hat wth Stick (H.H.)
Mounted Tom (M.T.)
Snare Drum (S.D.)
Floor Tom (F.T.)
Bass Drum (B.D.)
Hi-Hat with Foot (H.H.)

basic music notation review

Before starting this book, you need to know all of the following things that were taught in a beginning snare drum book.

If there's anything you don't remember, go back to that book and review it.

Once you are comfortable with all these things, you are ready to start with *Drumset 101*.

Getting Ready to Play

Counting

Clap your hands on beats 1, 2, 3 and 4.

Count:	1	2	3	4
	Clap	Clap	Clap	Clap

Reading Music Notation

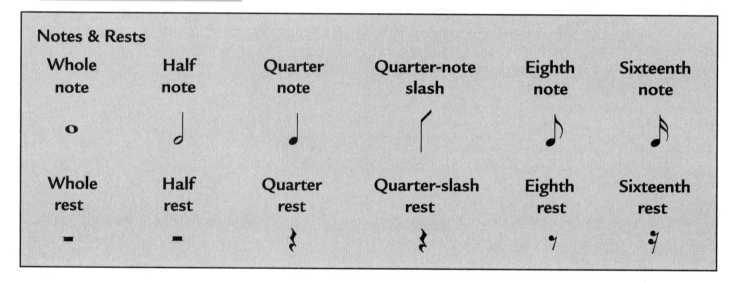

Notes & Rests

Whole note	Half note	Quarter note	Quarter-note slash	Eighth note	Sixteenth note
Whole rest	Half rest	Quarter rest	Quarter-slash rest	Eighth rest	Sixteenth rest

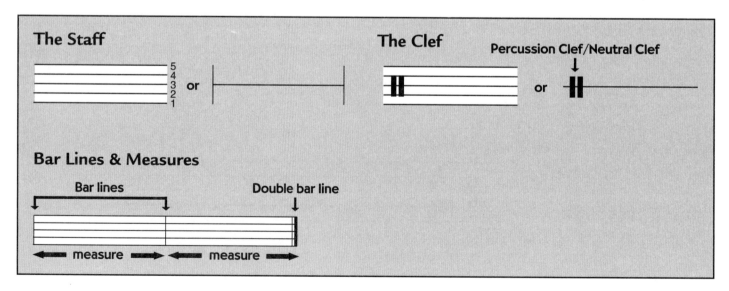

The Staff

5 4 3 2 1   or

The Clef

Percussion Clef/Neutral Clef

or

Bar Lines & Measures

Bar lines   Double bar line

measure   measure

Time Signatures

A $\frac{4}{4}$ *time signature* (called "four-four time") means there are four equal beats in every measure, and a quarter note ($\quarternote$) gets one beat.

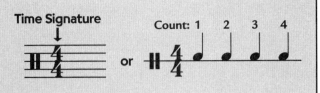

Repeat Sign

Double dots on the inside of a double barline mean to go back to the beginning and play again.

basic playing techniques

The Matched Grip

1. First, extend your right hand as if you were going to shake hands with someone.

2. Place the stick between your thumb and first finger at the fulcrum point (A).

3. Curve the other fingers around the stick (B).

4. Turn your hand over so your palm is facing towards the floor (C).

5. Repeat steps 1–4 with your left hand.

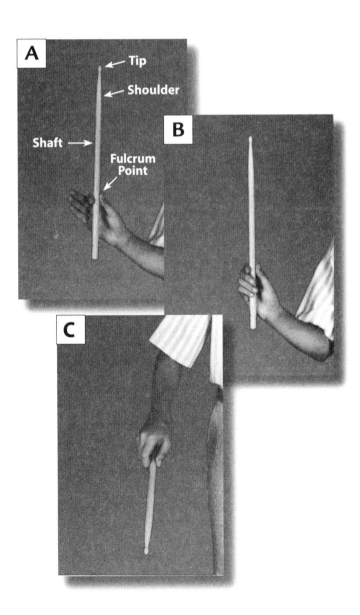

Striking the Drum

1. Hold the tip of the right stick above the drumhead.
2. Use the wrists (not the forearms) to lift the stick about four inches off the drum.
3. Drop the stick on the drum and let it return to the up position. It should strike near, but not on, the center of the drumhead.
4. Repeat, using the left stick.
5. Repeat, **slowly**, making sure that both sticks strike within the same beating area.

Striking the Ride Cymbal

1. First, extend your right hand as if you were going to shake hands.
2. Place the stick between your thumb and first finger (see matched grip).
3. Curve the other fingers around the stick (see matched grip).
4. Strike the cymbal about two inches from the edge.
5. Depending on the tempo and volume, the height of the stick producing the ride-cymbal stroke should be about four inches off the cymbal.

The Bass Drum

1. The bass drum is played with your right foot.

2. Play the bass drum using a *heel down* approach, which means keeping your foot flat on the foot board.

3. To play the bass-drum stroke, rock your foot until the beater strikes the head, then immediately return your foot to the up position. Do not leave the beater pressed up against the drumhead.

The Hi-Hat

1. The hi-hat is played with your left foot.

2. When at rest, the space between the cymbals should be about two inches.

3. When you press the foot pedal down, the cymbals come together.

4. When you play the hi-hat, use a rocking motion by stepping down on beats 2 & 4 (toe), and then rocking up on beats 1 & 3 (heel).

1 to 2 inches

Track 1

Practice Warm-up

Before playing along with the CD, practice the exercise alone until you are comfortable with it. Play it two times: the first time with drums, and the second without. Be sure to count!

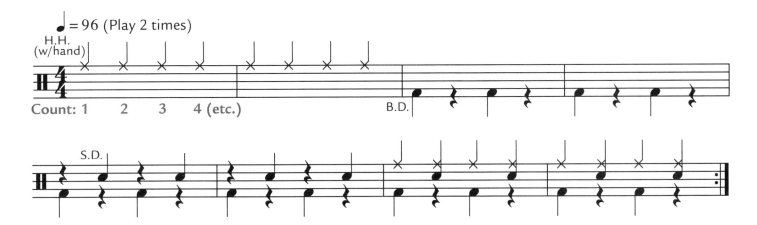

♩ = 96 (Play 2 times)

Jump Back
Track 2

Before playing along with the CD, practice this song alone until you are comfortable with it. Play it four times, and be sure to count! Concentrate on achieving a good balance of sound between the drums.

Practice Warm-up

Before playing along with the CD, practice this exercise alone until you are comfortable with it.
Play it two times: the first time with drums, and the second without. Be sure to count!

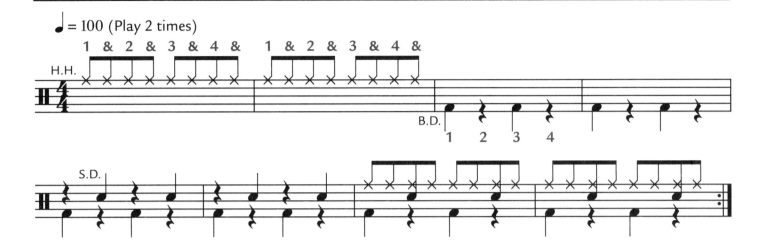

Howlin' Dog

Before playing along with the CD, practice this song alone until you are comfortable with it. Play it four times.

Medium rock (♩ = 108) (Play 4 times)

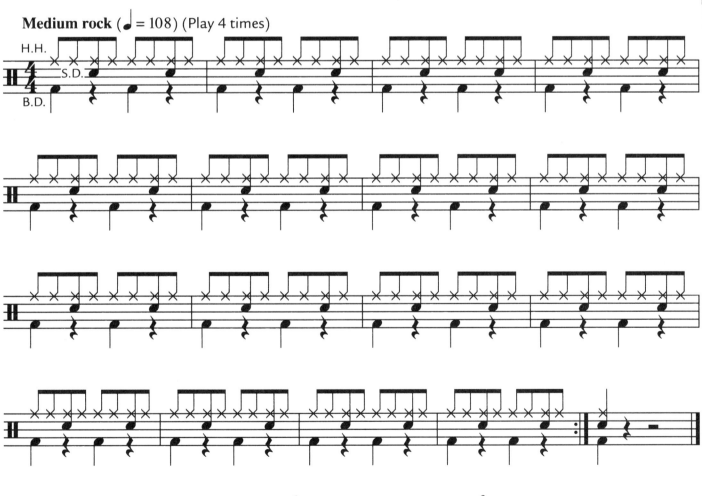

Alternate Bass Drum Patterns:

Drum Fills

A *drum fill* is a short, improvised solo played at the end of a musical phrase that serves as a bridge to connect ideas. Always practice fills in a musical *time** setting, playing three bars of time followed by the one-bar fill.

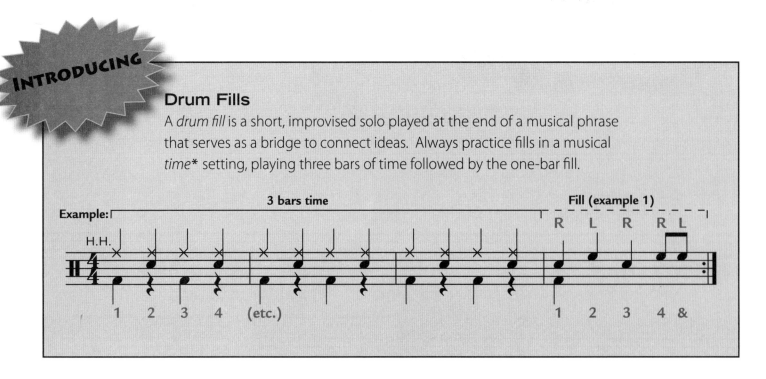

Play each fill exercise four times. Remember to always play three bars of time before you play each fill. Although fills break away from the basic beat, they should not speed up or slow down. Remember to count, and to pay attention to the stickings. The concept of the practice loop is to provide a steady pulse so that you do not rush or slow down during the bar of the fill.

Drum Fill Practice Loop

Track 5

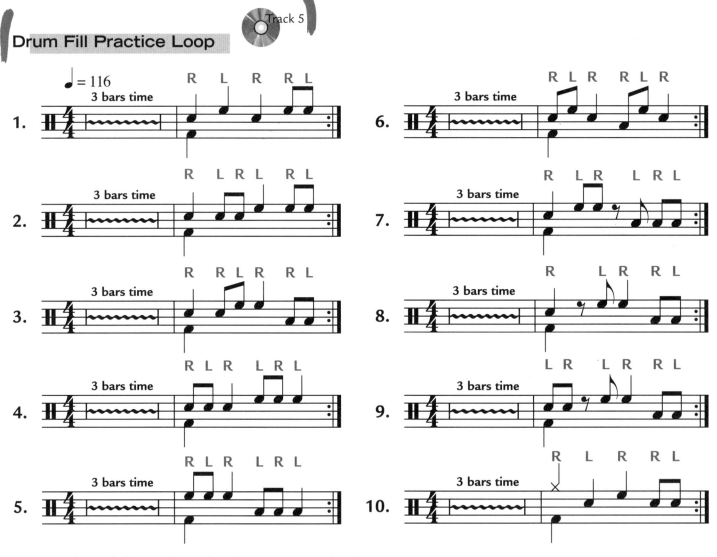

* Time is the underlying pulse within the music being played. For example, in track 5, the drum pattern is the time.

Trash Truck 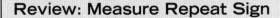 Track 6

Before playing along with the CD, practice the drum part alone until you are comfortable with it. Remember that the fills should not speed up or slow down. Play this song four times. You may use any of the fills on the previous page or, better yet, make up your own.

Medium rock (♩ = 120) (Play 4 times)

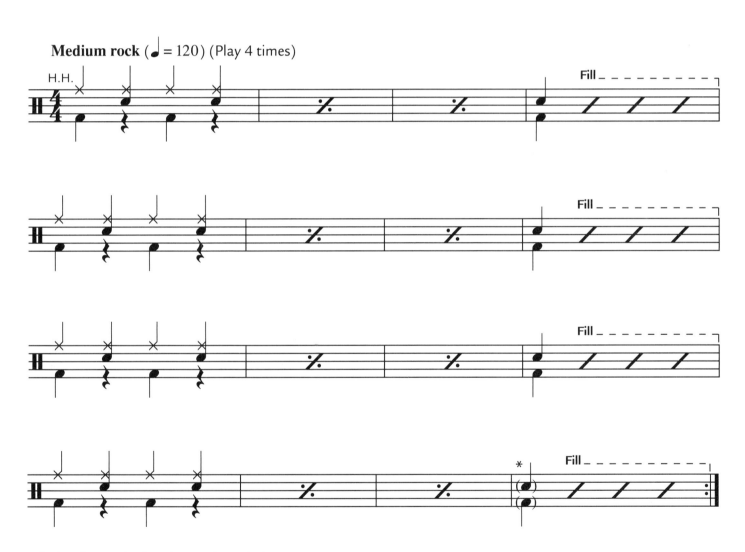

* End on beat 1 the fourth time through the song.

Alternate Hi-Hat Pattern: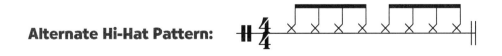

Spy Rock 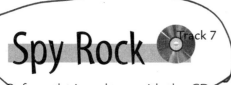 Track 7

Before playing along with the CD, practice this song alone until you are comfortable with it. Play it four times. Once you're comfortable with the written drum part, you may go back and create your own.

* End on beat 1 the fourth time through the song.

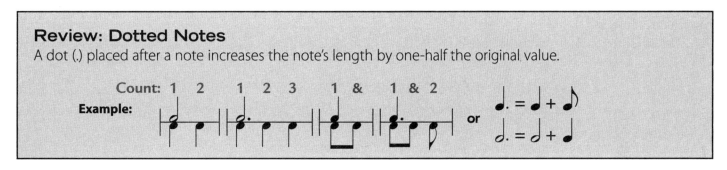

Review: Dotted Notes
A dot (.) placed after a note increases the note's length by one-half the original value.

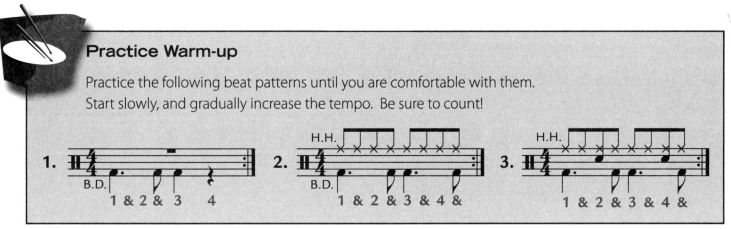

Practice Warm-up

Practice the following beat patterns until you are comfortable with them.
Start slowly, and gradually increase the tempo. Be sure to count!

Mozart Rocks!

Before playing along with the CD, practice this song alone until you are comfortable with it.
Play it four times.

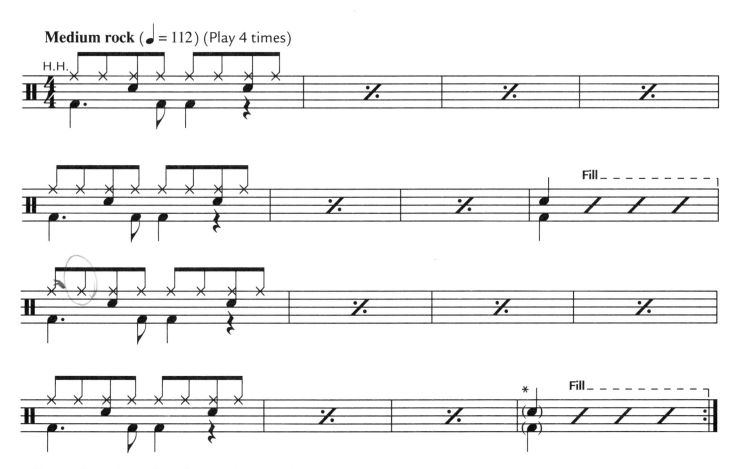

* End on beat 1 the fourth time through the song.

INTRODUCING

Two-Bar Fills

Play two bars of time followed by a two-bar fill. Play each fill exercise four times before moving on to the next one. Although fills break away from the basic beat, they should not speed up or slow down. Once you're comfortable with the written fills, you may create your own by adding additional toms.

Two-Bar Fill Practice Loop Track 9

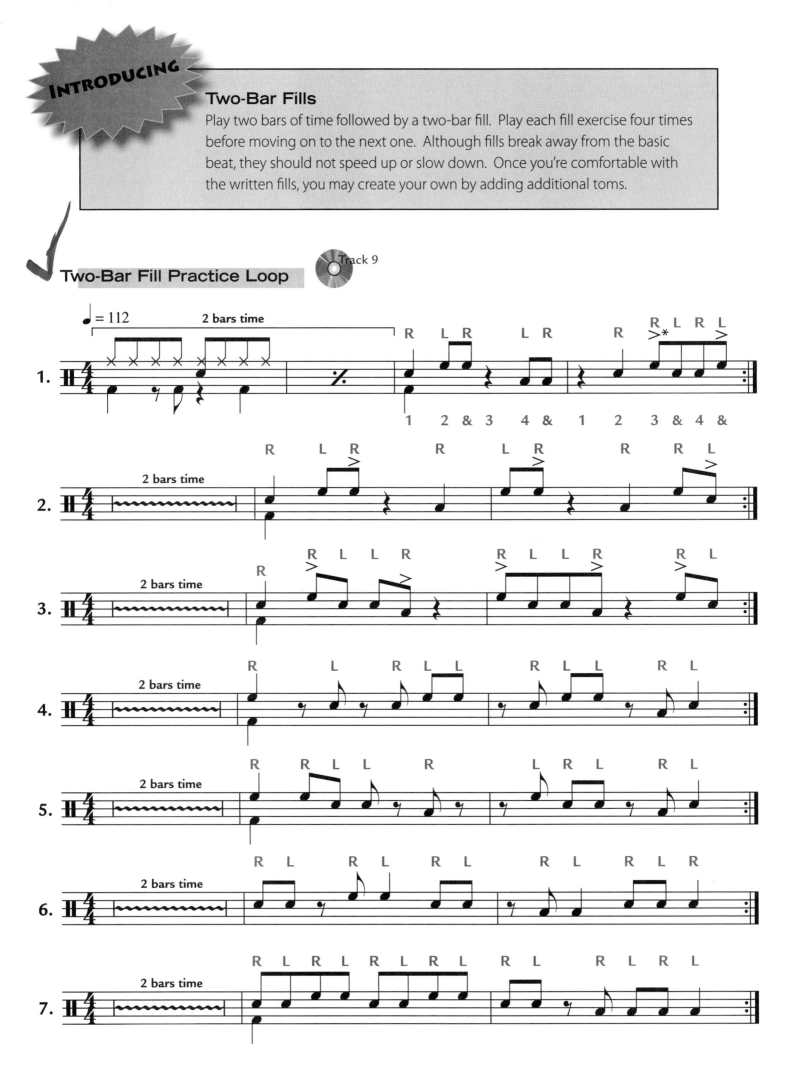

* > = Accent. Play the note a little louder.

Rockin' 1812 Overture

This song is played using a *half-time feel,* which means that the beat will feel half as fast as the original tempo. Before playing along with the CD, practice this song alone until you are comfortable with it.

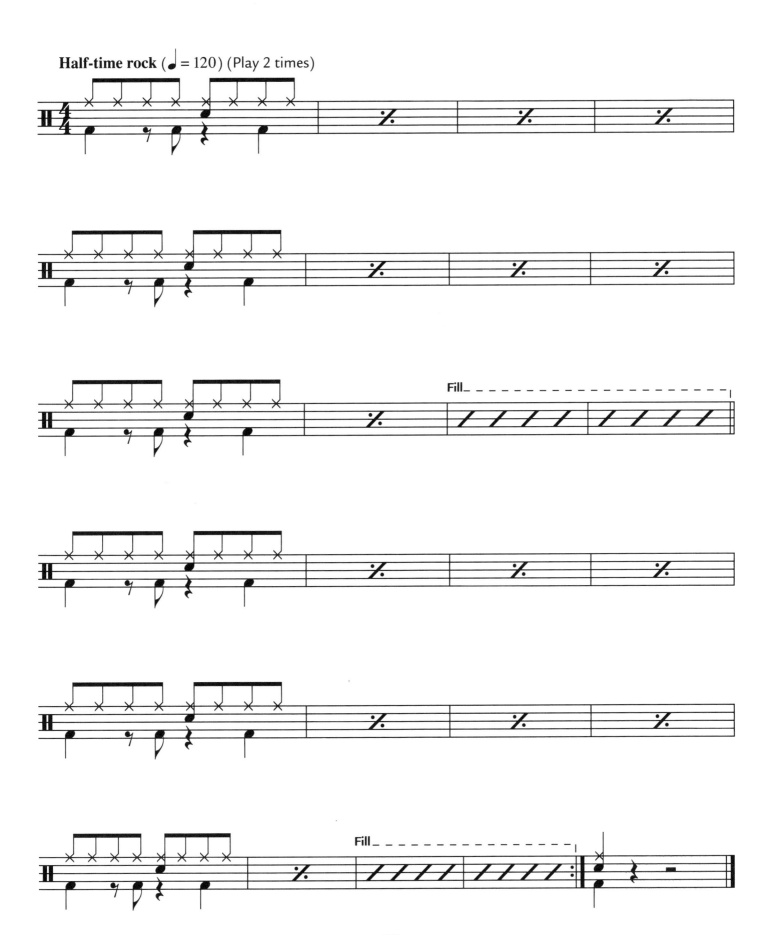

17

The Double Paradiddle and the Paradiddle-Diddle

When you play single strokes and double strokes together, both a sound pattern and a sticking pattern are created. One of these sticking patterns is called a *double paradiddle* and the other is called a *paradiddle-diddle*. Both are common drum rudiments.

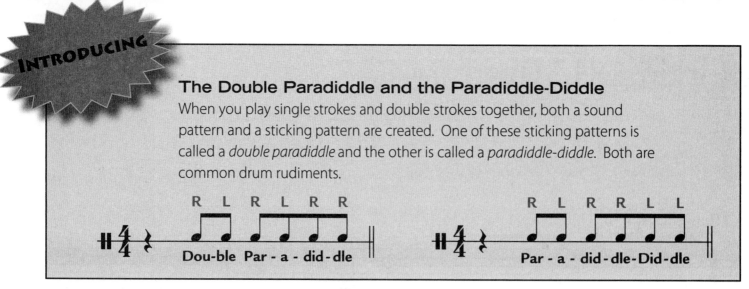

New Rudiment Practice Loop Track 11

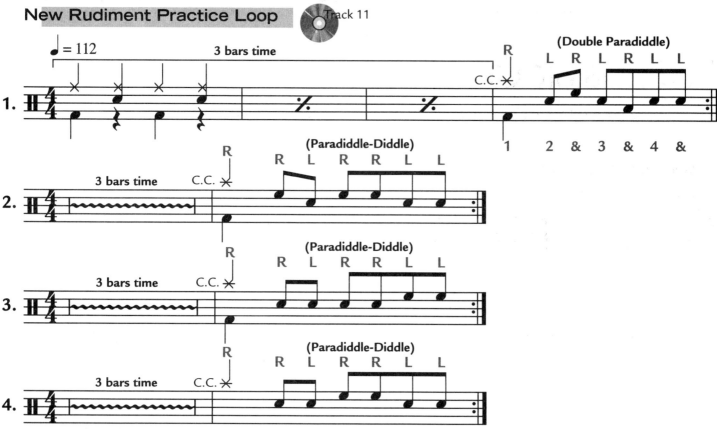

The Fermata

This symbol is a *fermata*. It is sometimes called a "bird's eye" because it looks like the eye of a bird. When you see a fermata over a note, play the note a little longer than it would normally be played. You should hold it about twice as long as usual. There is a fermata at the end of "Dad's Classic Car" on the following page.

Ties

A tie is a curved line that connects two notes. When two notes are tied, don't play the second note, but keep the first note playing until the second note is done. You are really adding the two notes together. There is a tie at the end of "Dad's Classic Car" on the following page.

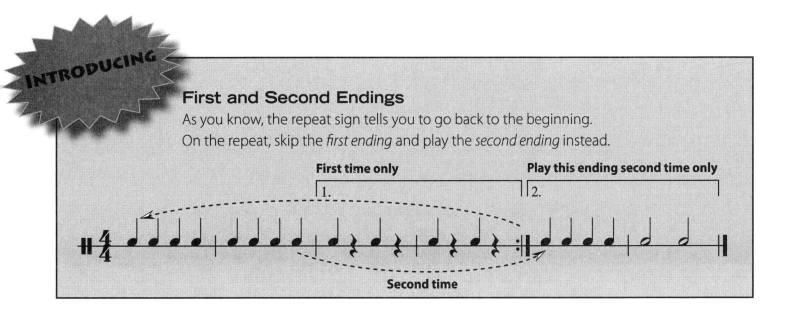

First and Second Endings

As you know, the repeat sign tells you to go back to the beginning.
On the repeat, skip the *first ending* and play the *second ending* instead.

Dad's Classic Car

Track 12

Before playing along with the CD, practice this song alone until you are comfortable with it.

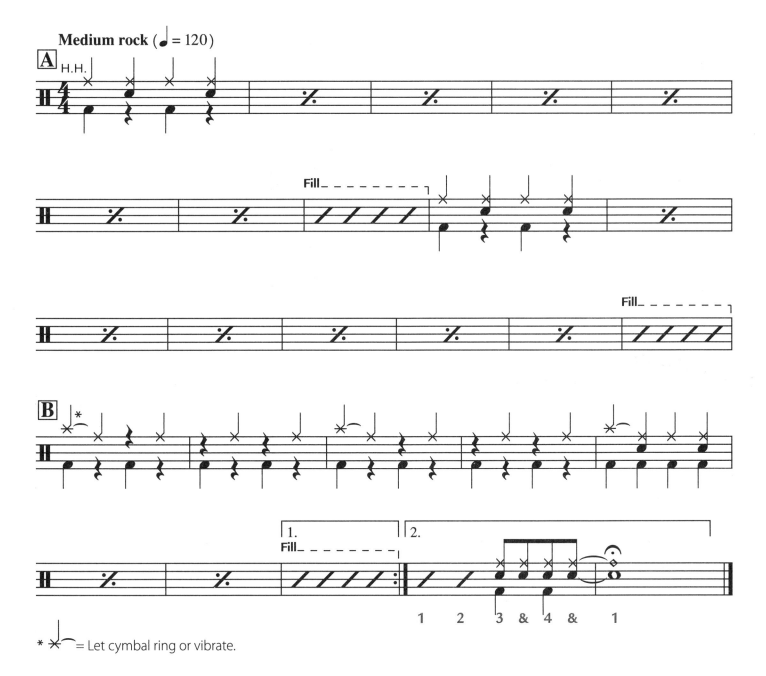

* ✗ = Let cymbal ring or vibrate.

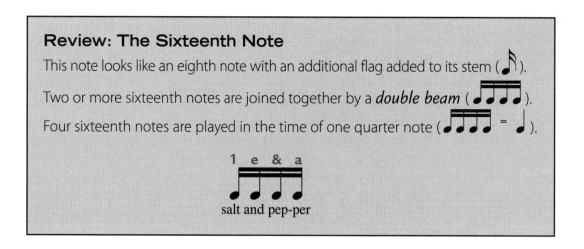
Funky Beat Track 13

Funk can be defined as a syncopated, sixteenth-note rock groove. In the following song, if you start the sixteenths in the right hand, the right hand moves to the snare drum on beats 2 & 4. It is reversed if you start with the left hand. Play this song two times.

Alternate Hi-Hat Pattern:

* A circle (o) represents an open hi-hat. When the hi-hat is in the open position, release the foot just enough so that the top cymbal slightly touches the bottom cymbal.

Practice Warm-up

Practice the following beats until you are comfortable with them. Start slowly, and gradually increase the tempo. Practice each beat at least eight times. Be sure to count.

1.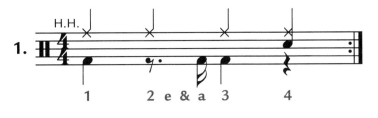

1   2 e & a 3   4

2.

3.

4.

Daisy Bell Track 14

"Daisy Bell" has been written using example 3 above. You can practice it using any of the above examples. Play this song three times. Be sure to count the measures and add fills at phrase points where indicated.

Medium funk rock (♩ = 84) (Play 3 times)

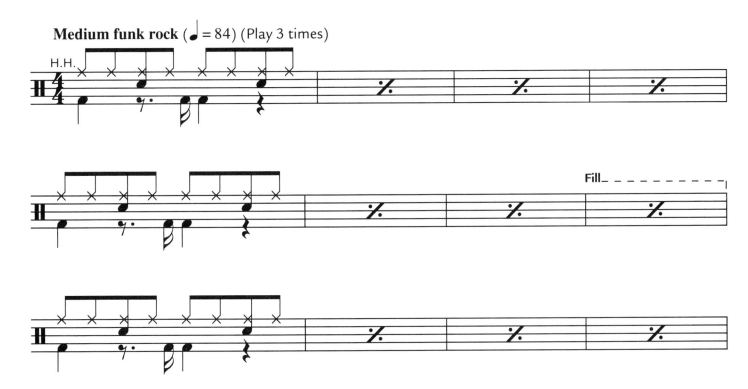

Hip-Hop #1

Track 15

Hip-Hop (sometimes referred to as a "funk shuffle") is a style of music popular among urban youth. Before playing along with the CD, practice this song alone until you are comfortable with it. Add fills when appropriate. In this particular style, the eighth and sixteenth notes should be played with a loose, swung feel.

* repeat the previous two bars.

Sixteenth-Note Fill Practice Loop

Play each fill exercise four times. Remember to always play three bars of time before you play each fill. Although fills break away from the basic beat, they should not speed up or slow down. Remember to count and pay attention to the stickings!

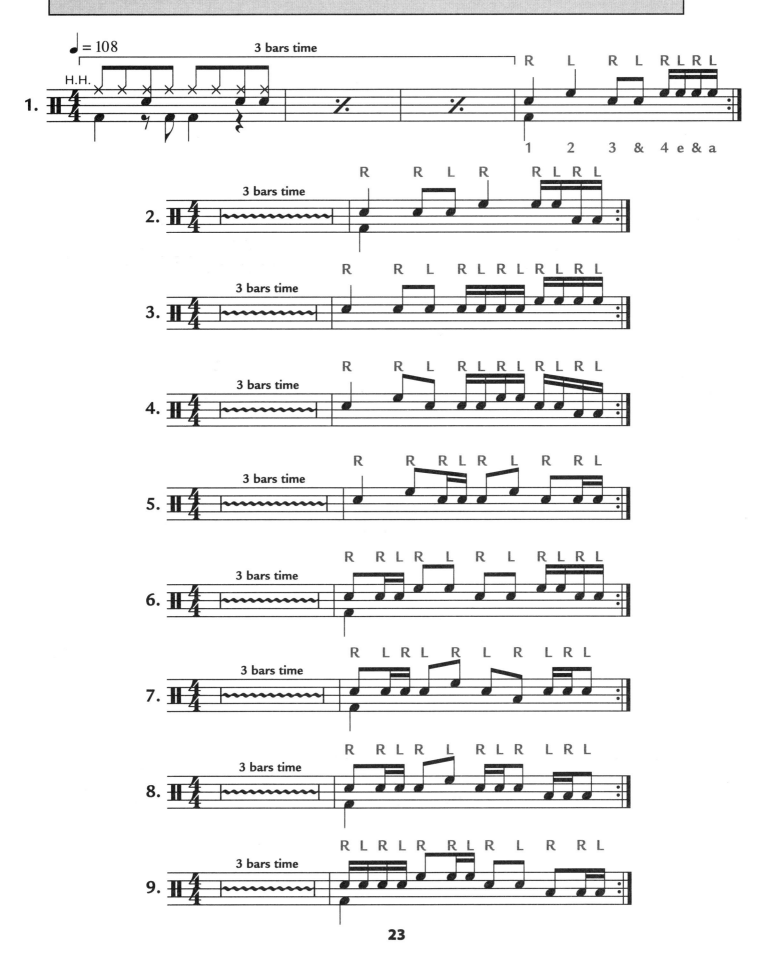

Boogie Blues

Track 17

Boogie is a style of rock music based on the blues. It is characterized by a repetitive bass figure.
Before playing along with the CD, practice this song alone until you are comfortable with it.
You may make up your own fills or use any of the previous fills you've learned.

* For songs with more than two endings, the number in the first bracket tells you how many times to go back to
   the beginning before moving on to the second bracket in order to finish the song.

Alternate Hi-Hat Sound:

Go back and play **Boogie Blues** with the hi-hat cymbals partially closed (cymbals lightly touching).
This will provide a looser, "swishing" sound.

Practice Warm-up

Practice the following beat patterns until you are comfortable with them. Start slowly, and gradually increase the tempo. Practice each beat at least eight times.

Let's Dance Track 18

Before playing along with the CD, practice this song alone until you are comfortable with it.
Add fills when appropriate.

* Play these three notes on the sixth time only.

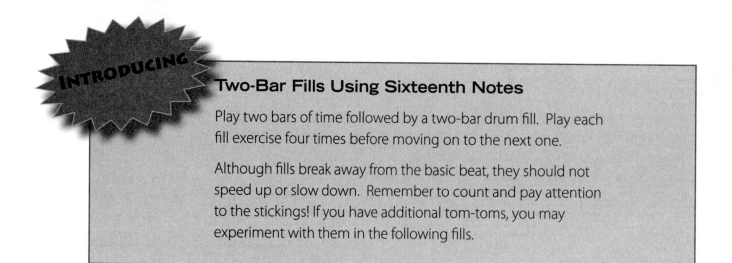

Two-Bar Fills Using Sixteenth Notes

Play two bars of time followed by a two-bar drum fill. Play each fill exercise four times before moving on to the next one.

Although fills break away from the basic beat, they should not speed up or slow down. Remember to count and pay attention to the stickings! If you have additional tom-toms, you may experiment with them in the following fills.

Two-Bar Fill Practice Loop Track 19

Flyin' High  Track 20

Before playing along with the CD, practice this song
alone until you are comfortable with it. Play the entire
song, including repeats, three times.

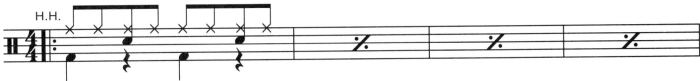

Syncopation

Notes that are played between the main beats of a measure and held across the beat are called *syncopated* notes. In the following rhythm, the first quarter note is syncopated because it is played on "&" and held across beat 2.

Syncopation also occurs when a note that is one beat or longer starts on an "&". In this example, the first note is syncopated because it is one beat long and starts on "&".

Practice the following rhythms separately until you are comfortable with them.

Start slowly, and gradually increase the tempo.

Remember to count carefully and to keep a steady pulse!

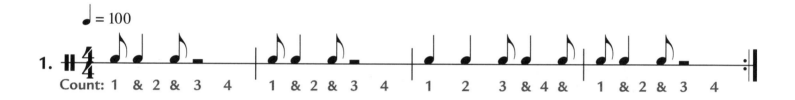

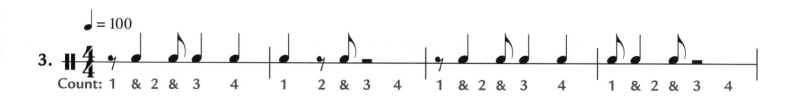

Half-Time Rock

Track 21

Before playing along with the CD, practice the
song alone until you are comfortable with it.
Play this song four times.

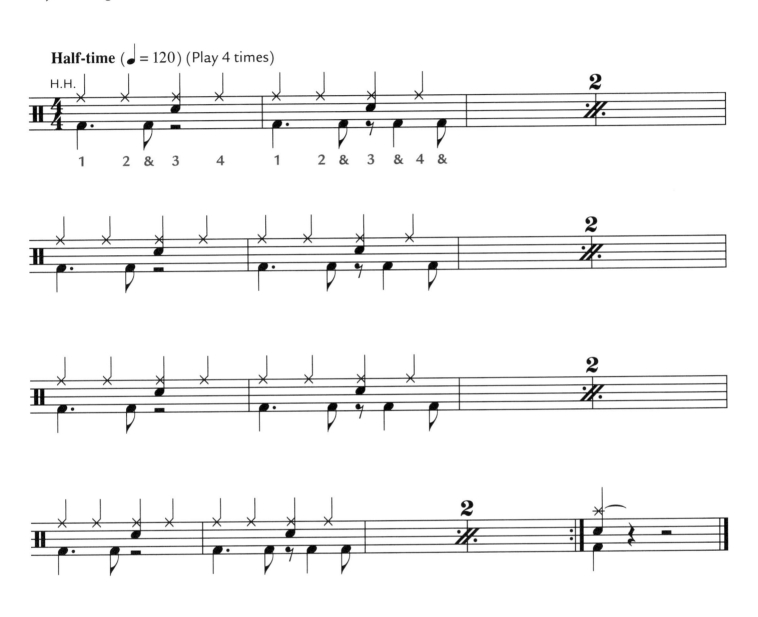

Alternate Hi-Hat Patterns:

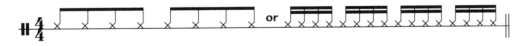

Alternate Bass Drum Patterns:

Hip-Hop #2

Before playing along with the CD, practice this song alone
until you are comfortable with it. Add fills when appropriate.
In this particular style, the eighth and sixteenth notes should
be played with a loose, swung feel.

Alternate Hi-Hat Pattern:

* Play only the second time through the song.

Cruisin'  Track 23

Before playing along with the CD, practice this song alone until you are comfortable with it. You may play either of the two versions below along with the CD. Remember to play the accented notes a little louder. When you are comfortable with the part, go back and add fills to bars 7 & 8. Play this song nine times.

Bright fusion ($\quarternote$ = 132) (Play 9 times)

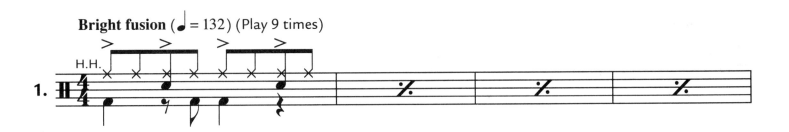

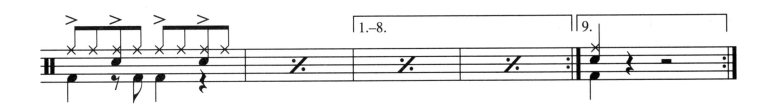

$\quarternote$ = 132 (Play 9 times)

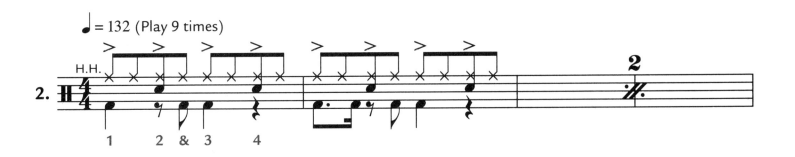

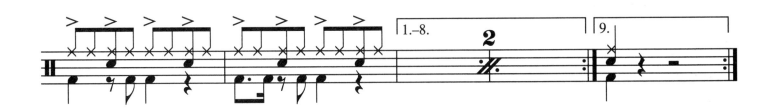

Alternate Hi-Hat Pattern:

A Brief History of the Bossa Nova

Latin-American music is dance music. The bossa nova originated in Brazil and immigrated to American jazz in the 1960s. It has a light feel and a somewhat repetitive, hypnotic groove. The composer considered to be the godfather of the bossa nova is Antonio Carlos Jobim.

INTRODUCING

The Cross-Stick

To produce the *cross-stick* sound, leave the tip of the stick resting on the drumhead, lift the butt-end of the stick, and strike the rim of the drum. It is notated like this:

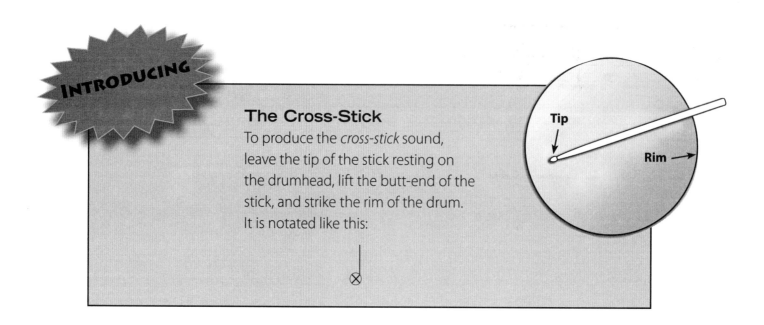

Performance Tips

1. When playing the cross-stick pattern, make sure the stick is in the proper position so that it doesn't produce a thin sound.
2. The overall volume between the hands and feet should be balanced.
3. Rhythms should be played consistently and accurately.

The Bossa Nova Rhythm

The basic feel of the bossa nova comes from playing straight eighth notes on either the ride cymbal or hi-hat, and dotted quarter/eighth-note rhythms on the bass drum. The snare drum cross-stick rhythm imitates the clave rhythm.

Practice Warm-up

Before playing along with the CD, practice each exercise alone until you are comfortable with them. Play each two times: the first time with drums, and the second without. Be sure to count!

Cheater Bossa Track 24

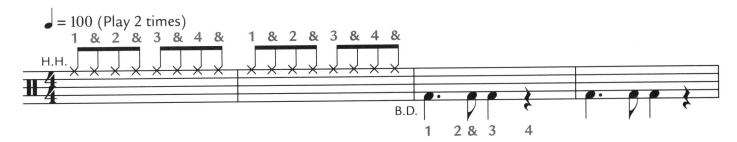

Basic Bossa Track 25

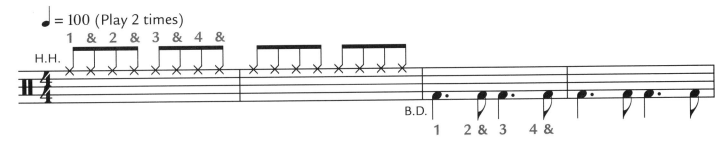

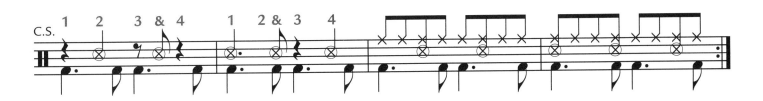

Latin Independence Exercises

While playing the same ride cymbal/hi-hat pattern with your right hand and the bass drum pattern with your right foot, play the following cross-stick rhythms with your left hand. Play each exercise along with Track 26 at least four times. This will help develop independence between your arms and legs. Remember to count carefully and keep a steady pulse!

If you played the eighth-note ride pattern on the hi-hat, go back and play the exercises using the ride cymbal, and add the hi-hat on beats 2 & 4.

Medium Bossa Nova Track 27

Before playing along with the CD, practice this song alone until you are comfortable with it. Add fills when appropriate. The drum pattern for this bossa nova has been simplified. For that reason, it is sometimes referred to as the "cheater bossa."

If you played the eighth-note ride pattern on the hi-hat, go back and play the song using the ride cymbal, and add the hi-hat on beats 2 & 4 .

Brazilian Holiday

Track 28

Before playing along with the CD, practice this song alone until you are comfortable with it. Add fills when appropriate, and make sure you play the rhythms consistently and accurately.

If you played the eighth-note ride pattern on the hi-hat, go back and play the song using the ride cymbal, and add the hi-hat on beats 2 & 4.

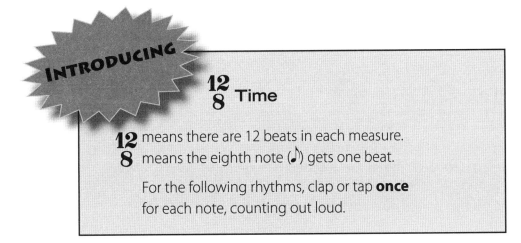

$\frac{12}{8}$ Time

12 means there are 12 beats in each measure.

8 means the eighth note ($\flat$) gets one beat.

For the following rhythms, clap or tap **once** for each note, counting out loud.

Dotted quarter note ($\bullet\cdot$)

or rests ($\xi\ \gamma$) or ($\xi\cdot$) = 3 beats

Quarter note ($\bullet$)

or quarter rest (ξ) = 2 beats

Eighth note ($\flat$)

or eighth rest (γ) = 1 beat

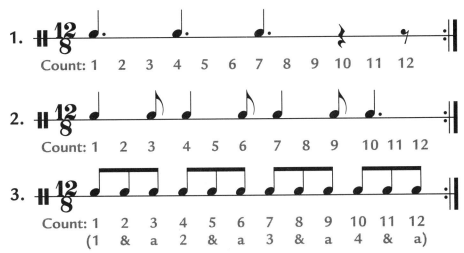

Track 29

Practice Warm-up

The following exercises will help you develop the skills needed to play a style of music called *rhythm and blues* (R&B), a folk-based style of popular music performed principally by African-American musicians between the late 1940s and the early 1960s. R&B was the forerunner of rock, and is still very popular today. Practice the following exercises alone until you are comfortable with them. Start slowly and gradually increase the tempo. Play each exercise, along with Track 29, at least four times.

Sweetheart Blues 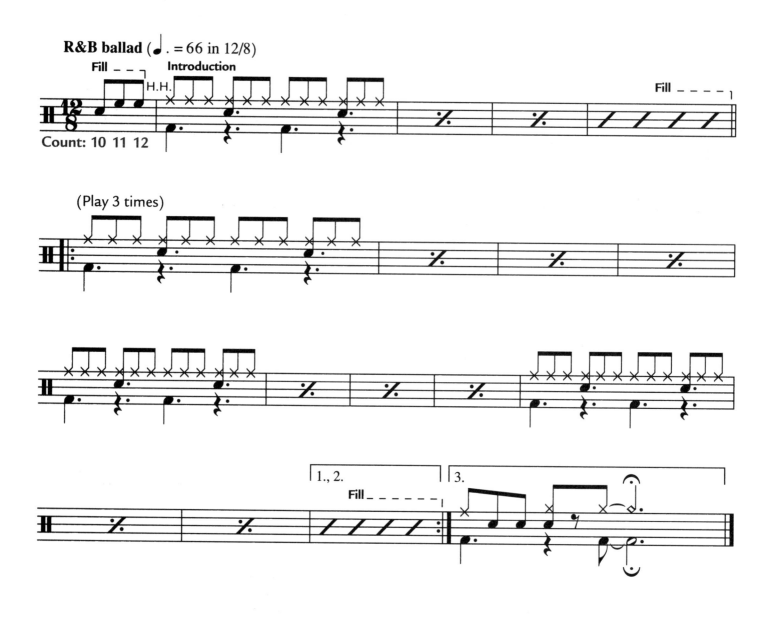 Track 30

Before playing along with the CD, practice this song alone until
you are comfortable with it. You may play any of the beats on the
previous page with this song. When comfortable with the part, go
back and add fills at the various phrase points where indicated.

Alternate Hi-Hat Pattern:

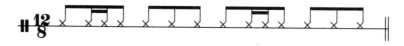

Alternate Bass Drum Pattern:

America, the Beautiful  Track 31

This song was once again popularized by the late, great R&B singer Ray Charles.
Before playing along with the CD, practice this alone until you are comfortable with it.

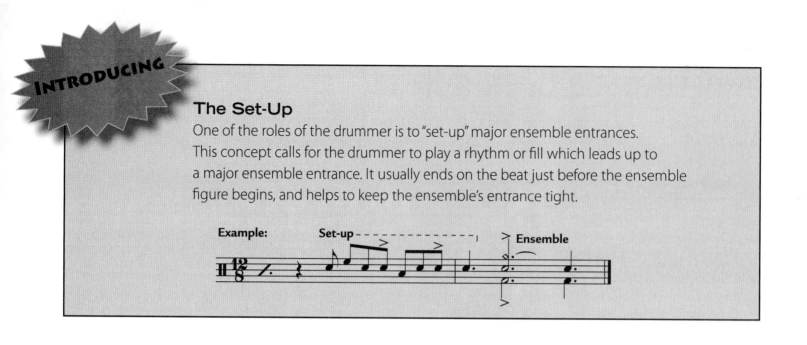

The Set-Up

One of the roles of the drummer is to "set-up" major ensemble entrances.
This concept calls for the drummer to play a rhythm or fill which leads up to
a major ensemble entrance. It usually ends on the beat just before the ensemble
figure begins, and helps to keep the ensemble's entrance tight.

Swingin' Hard Track 32

Before playing along with the CD, practice this song alone
until you are comfortable with it. Play it four times.

* Create your own fill.

The Shuffle

The shuffle feel is the rhythmic impetus of rhythm and blues. It is a form of swing, and is based on the triplet subdivision. Much like rock, it relies on pattern repetition and a pronounced emphasis on beats 2 & 4. The shuffle evokes the feeling of a locomotive engine, tirelessly chugging along.

Shuffling Along Track 33

Before playing along with the CD, practice this song alone until you are comfortable with it. In this particular style, the focus should be on a strong 2 & 4 backbeat.

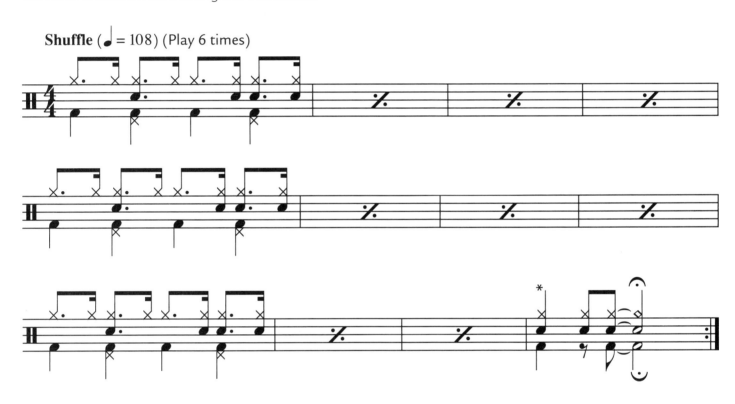

If you played the dotted eighth and sixteenth-note ride pattern on the ride cymbal, go back and play the song on the hi-hat.

* Play only the sixth time through the song.

Jazz

Jazz is a style of music that was created in the United States. What makes jazz sound like jazz?

1. The melody is often *embellished* (has added details), *syncopated* (see page 28 for definition), or *varied* at the performer's discretion.

2. The harmony may include more *dissonant* (clashing) notes.

3. The rhythm emphasizes beats 2 & 4, which gives it a "swing" feel.

4. Jazz musicians compose new melodies on the spot, which is called *improvisation*.

Triplets

A *triplet* is a group of three notes of equal value, usually played in the place of one note. Triplets have a numeral "3" placed above or beneath the center note.

The Basic Jazz Ride Rhythm

The basic feel in jazz drumming comes from the cymbals, specifically the *ride rhythm* played by the right hand on the ride cymbal, and the hi-hat played most often on beats 2 & 4. The ride rhythm is based on a triplet feel, as shown in the second example.

Ride-Cymbal Pattern 1

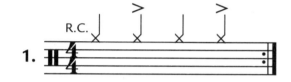

Ride-Cymbal Pattern 2

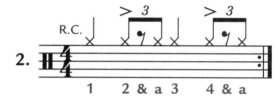

Track 34

Snare Drum Independence Exercises

While playing either of the ride-cymbal patterns above with your right hand, play the following exercises on the snare drum with your left hand. Play each exercise along with Track 34 at least four times.

Once you're comfortable with playing the ride cymbal and snare drum together, go back
and play the examples above, adding the hi-hat on beats 2 & 4 as in the following examples.

Quarter-Note Ride Pattern with Hi-Hat and Snare

1.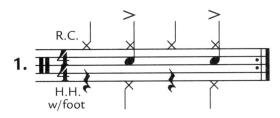

Triplet Ride Pattern with Hi-Hat and Snare

2.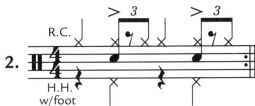

Track 34

Bass Drum Independence Exercises

Ride-Cymbal Pattern 1

1.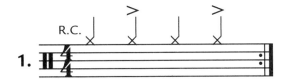

Ride-Cymbal Pattern 2

2.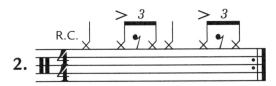

While playing either of the ride-cymbal patterns above with your right hand, play the following exercises
on the bass drum with your right foot. Play each exercise along with Track 34 at least two times.

♩ = 100

1.

4.

2.

5.

3.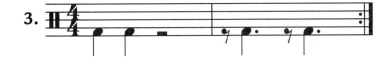

6.

Once you're comfortable with playing the ride cymbal and bass drum together, go back and
play the examples above, adding the hi-hat on beats 2 & 4 as in the following examples.

Quarter-Note Ride Pattern with Hi-Hat and Bass Drum

1.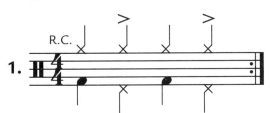

Triplet Ride Pattern with Hi-Hat and Bass Drum

2.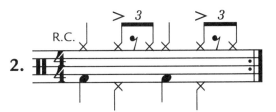

43

Jazz Independence Warm-up

Play the following exercise, which combines both hands and both feet.

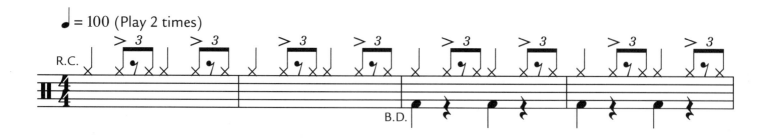

A Swing and a Miss Track 36

Before playing along with the CD, practice the part alone until you are comfortable with it. You may play any of the previous jazz patterns or independence rhythms along with this song. Play this song six times.

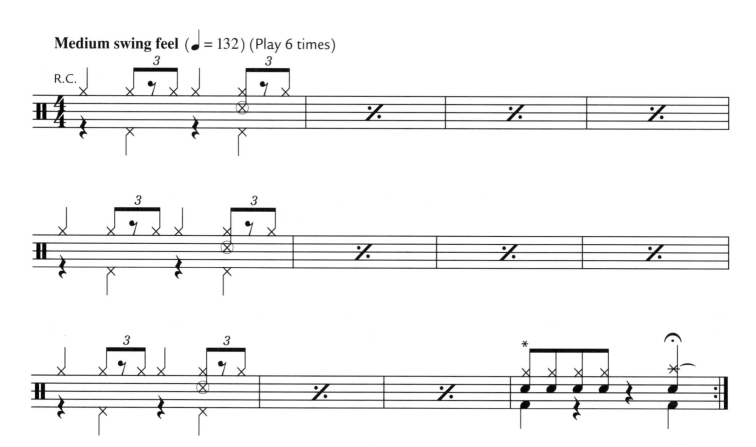

* Play on the sixth time only.

Snare Drum & Bass Drum Independence Exercises

While playing the ride-cymbal pattern (below) with your right hand and the hi-hat on beats 2 & 4 with your left foot, play the following snare drum and bass drum patterns. Play each exercise along with Track 34 or 37 at least four times. This will help develop independence between your hands and feet. Remember to count carefully and keep a steady pulse!

45

Jazz Fills

As in rock, a jazz fill is a short, improvised solo played at the end of a musical phrase that serves as a bridge to connect ideas. Always practice fills in a musical time setting, playing three bars of time followed by the one-bar fill. Pay close attention to the accents and stickings.

One-Bar Jazz Fill Practice Loop   Track 38

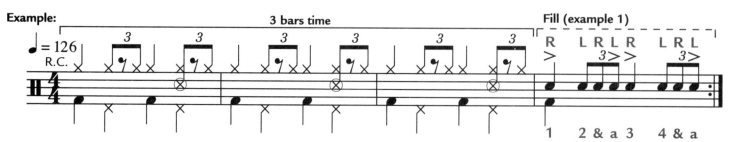

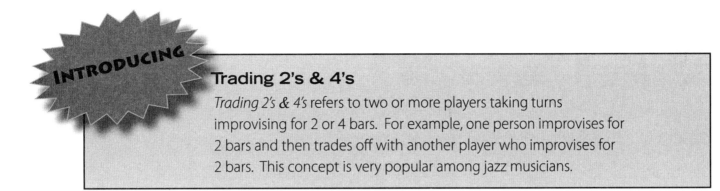

Trading 2's & 4's

Trading 2's & 4's refers to two or more players taking turns improvising for 2 or 4 bars. For example, one person improvises for 2 bars and then trades off with another player who improvises for 2 bars. This concept is very popular among jazz musicians.

Tradin' the Blues Track 39

Before playing along with the CD, practice this song alone until you are comfortable with it. At letter B, the piano and drums will trade 2's. Once you're comfortable with using the cross-stick, experiment with some of the previous snare drum and bass drum independence ideas.

* Once you are comfortable with the written fills, go back and make up your own.

Catch Me If You Can 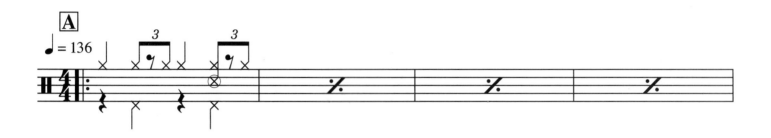 Track 40

Before playing along with the CD, practice this song alone until you are comfortable with it.
At letter B, the piano and drums will trade 4's. Make up your own solo fills.

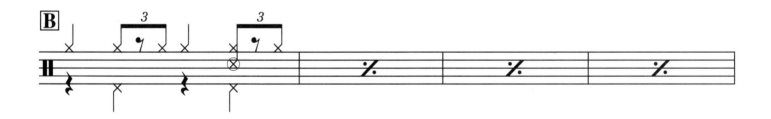

(Repeat 7 times)

Solo fill

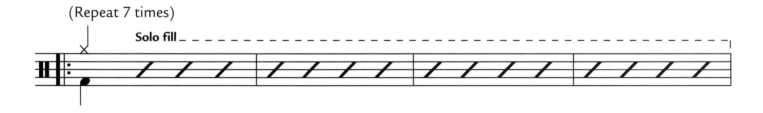

* Play this rhythm the seventh time